CHINESE COOKING

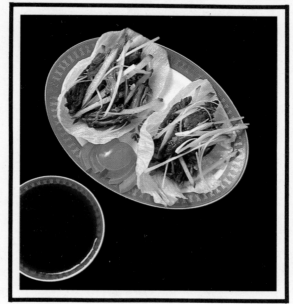

CONTENTS

NEW YORK

INTRODUCTION

To write about Chinese cooking is to introduce the Westerner to some of the basic realities of China – the colour and flavour of Chinese life. The cuisine of China so reflects the actual country that to write of Chinese cooking is to write about China herself. The vast range of dishes – for everyday meals, family dinners or festival celebrations – varies with the seasons and with all the different provinces and regions spread over this massive country. Each place has its own, inimitable flavours. From the food of the market-place, the tea-house or the run-down country temples to the more sophisticated specialities of the restaurants – the elegant Peking Duck, the seafood specialities of the East or the spicy delights of Szechuan – this book sets out to capture the diversity that is indeed the wonder of this Oriental cuisine.

The Chinese, as a nation, have accumulated over many thousands of years an incredible wealth of experience in cooking and food preparation and have developed a natural cuisine which is characteristically their own.

There are at least 5000 well-known Chinese dishes, each with its own distinctive combination of flavour, fragrance and texture, which have caused their cooking to enjoy such a high international reputation. Even those who know of the variety that exists may be suprised to learn that there are 5 major schools of cookery. Each commands its own area of influence – the Peking school in the North East, the Fukienese in the East, the Cantonese in the South West, the Honan in the centre and Szechuan to the West.

Peking, the cultural centre, introduced the art of lavish entertainment. Peking, where the kings and princes, noblemen and scholars, wealthy and middle classes gathered, gave birth to the great Peking chefs – there to please these sophisticated palates. Today, the sum of their efforts lies in the mild and light preparations that are the epitome of elegance.

The coastal province of Fukien is the home of the fisher folk. Its dishes reflect the proximity to the sea and seafood, especially fish, is prominent in their cooking. Soups too are a speciality of this region; no Fukien menu is complete without soups – sometimes as many as eight during a banquet.

Cantonese cooking is the one that is the most widely known; the food has a variety that would astound any gourmet for it covers almost every available ingredient. Of all the schools, this is probably the only one to insist on food being served as close to its original state as possible. As a result, its followers have had to master the stir-fry method of cooking that is unique to Chinese cuisine.

Honan's chief contribution comes in the form of the popular sweet-sour dishes, whereas Szechuan food has the high level of spiciness that could well surprise a seasoned Indian palate! In the summer, Szechuan is a very hot country. It is not surprising therefore that its people like their food hot and peppery, as in many tropical areas. And so, from the thousands of recipes created throughout the years, comes this small selection. The chosen dishes are not necessarily the most popular, but rather those which best convey the excellence of this cuisine.

Belonging to one of the most creative civilizations of all time, the Chinese have incorporated inventiveness into every aspect of their life, indeed, this has become the keynote of their world-renowned cuisine.

Wonton Soup with Watercress and Crispy Wonton

Shark's Fin Soup

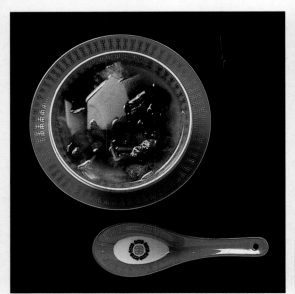

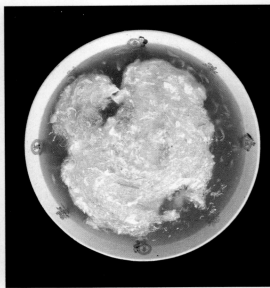

Wonton Soup with Watercress and Cripsy Wonton

1 bunch watercress	½ tsp ground ginger
½ lb ground pork	¼ lb ready made wonton
1) 1 tbsp soy sauce	wrappers
1 tsp sesame oil	5 cups chicken broth
½ tsp sugar	1 tsp salt
1 tbsp white wine	1 tsp soy sauce
½ tsp pepper	1 tsp sesame oil

Chop half watercress. Place in individual soup bowls. Rinse the other half in boiling water. Finely chop. Mix with the ground pork and 1). Marinate for 5-6 minutes. Blend well. Place ½ tsp mixture below the centre of each wonton wrapper. Fold one side over the filling. Moisten the corners with water, fold over to seal. Repeat until all mixture is used.

In a deep pan, bring 4 pints water to a boil, add the wontons, bring to a boil, cook for 5 minutes. Bring the chicken broth to a boil, add salt and soy sauce to taste. Transfer wontons to the soup, add sesame oil and pour into watercress lined bowls.

Shark's Fin Soup

½ cup shark's fin	1 cup crab meat
3-4 slices ginger root	½ lb cooked chicken meat,
8 Chinese dried mushrooms	shredded
2 pints chicken broth	2 tbsp cornstarch blended in
1 tsp salt	tbsp water
1 tbsp dark soy sauce	½ tsp sesame oil

Soak shark's fin overnight. Drain, simmer in 2 pints water with shredded ginger root for 1½ hours. Drain. Simmer again in fresh water for 45 minutes. Remove and drain.

Soak mushrooms overnight. Drain. Remove stems quarter caps. Heat broth in a ceramic pot. When boiling add mushrooms and fins. Simmer for 15 minutes. Add salt, soy sauce, and crab meat. Bring to a boil. Boil for 2-3 minutes. Add shredded chicken, and cornstarch mixture. Bring to a boil. Stir for 3-4 minutes. Sprinkle with sesame oil and serve.

Duck Carcass Soup

At the end of a Peking Duck dinner, it is customary to serve this soup which simply consists of the duck carcass, water and a few simple ingredients.

½ Chinese cabbage	1 tbsp vinegar
2 cakes bean curd	5 cups water
2 tbsp soy sauce	

Cut the cabbage into 2″ pieces. Cut the bean curd into ½″ pieces. Place the duck carcass in a large pan with the cabbage, bean curd, soy sauce and vinegar. Add cold water to cover. Bring to a boil. Simmer for 30 minutes. Remove carcass and serve soup.

Duck Carcass Soup

SOUPS

Peking Sliced Lamb with Cucumber Soup

Chicken, Ham & Sweetcorn Soup

Peking Sliced Lamb with Cucumber Soup

½ lb leg of lamb, bone removed	1½ tsp sesame oil
	5 cups chicken broth
5″ piece cucumber	salt and pepper
1 tbsp soy sauce	1½ tbsp wine vinegar

Cut the lamb into wafer thin slices. Thinly slice the cucumber. Sprinkle the lamb with the soy sauce and sesame oil. Marinate for 15 minutes.

Season the broth with salt and pepper. Bring to a boil. Add the sliced lamb. Poach in the broth for 1 minute. Remove with a slotted spoon. Poach the cucumber in the broth for 2 minutes. Return the lamb, stir in the vinegar, adjust seasoning and serve.

Chicken, Ham & Sweetcorn Soup

1 chicken breast	¼ cup water
2 egg whites	3 tbsp chopped scallion
3¾ cups chicken broth	1 tsp salt
1 (7 oz) can sweetcorn kernels	1 thin slice cooked smoked ham
1 tbsp cornstarch	

Finely chop the chicken flesh, mix with the egg white. Bring the broth to a boil in a large pan. Add the sweetcorn, then the cornstarch mixed with the water. Reboil the mixture, add the chicken and egg white. Add the scallions and salt. Simmer for 5 minutes. Pour the soup into a heated tureen, garnish with finely chopped ham.

Shanghai Spare ribs

2 lbs pork spare ribs	2 tbsp pale dry sherry
Marinade:	1 tsp garlic, minced
¼ cup soy sauce	pepper
2 tbsp sugar	ground ginger
2 tbsp Hoisin sauce	2 tbsp chicken stock or water

Place spare ribs in a large, shallow ovenproof pan. In a small bowl mix all the other ingredients together. Pour over the spare ribs and marinate for 3-4 hours. Turn and baste every hour or so. Cover dish tightly with foil. Cook at 375° for 45 mins. Uncover, baste with sauce, raise temperature to 425°. Cook for a further 15-20 minutes. Baste and turn occasionally until dark brown. Serve.

Shanghai
Spare ribs

SOUPS/MEAT

Shanghai Long-cooked Knuckle of Pork

Stir-fry Beef with Mango Slices

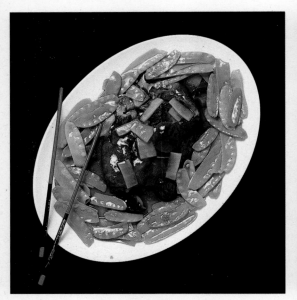

Shanghai Long-cooked Knuckle of Pork

3-4 lb pork hock	¼ cup sugar
7½ cups water	½ cup pale dry sherry
3 scallions	4 slices ginger root
½ cup soy sauce	2 tbsp lard

Clean the pork, slash with a knife to ease cooking. Place in a deep pan, add the water. Bring to a boil, simmer for 15 minutes. Discard ⅓ of the water. Cut the scallions into 1″ sections. Add the scallions, soy sauce, sugar, sherry, ginger and lard to the pork. Cover and simmer for 2 hours. Turn the pork over several times during cooking. By the end of the cooking time the water in the pan should have reduced to a ¼. Bring to a boil to reduce again by half. The broth will have become rich and brown. Place the pork in a deep bowl. Pour the broth over. Serve with steamed vegetables and rice.

Stir-fry Beef with Mango Slices

½ lb fillet of beef	1 tbsp soy sauce
1 large mango	1 tsp cornstarch
1 tbsp (shredded) ginger root	¼ tsp sugar
1 tbsp (shredded) scallions	¼ tsp pepper
1) 1 tbsp cooking wine	

Cut beef into thin bite-sized slices. Marinate in 1) for 20 minutes. Skin mango, cut into ¼″ thick slices. Set wok over a high heat, pour 4 tbsp oil into the wok, wait until it's almost smoking. Reduce heat to moderate, stir fry the beef and ginger for 1-2 minutes. Remove with a slotted spoon. Toss the mango slices in the hot oil for a few seconds, return the beef and ginger, and scallions. Stir over the heat for a further few seconds. Serve immediately.

Szechuan 'Yu Hsiang' Pork Ribbons Quick Fried with Shredded Vegetables

¾ lb lean pork	1 cup bean sprouts
3 slices ginger root	4 tbsp oil
2 cloves garlic	1 tsp salt
¼ cup Szechuan Hot Ja Chai pickle	3 tsp sesame oil
1 cup snow peas	4 tbsp broth
1 cup white cabbage	Sauce:
1 red capsicum	3 tbsp soy sauce
2 young carrots	2 tbsp Hoisin sauce
2 dried chilli peppers	1 tbsp chilli sauce
	2 tbsp vinegar

Cut pork into very thin slices. Cut again into 1″ strips. Cut ginger, garlic, pickle, snow peas, cabbage, capsicum, carrots and chillies into small slices. Mix together the sauce ingredients.

Heat the 4 tbsp oil in a wok. When hot, add the chillies, pickle, pork and ginger. Stir over a high heat for 2 minutes. Add all the shredded vegetables and bean sprouts. Sprinkle with salt, stir over the heat for 2 minutes. Add the broth, stir for 2 minutes more. Add the sauce ingredients, and sesame oil, stirring for a further 2 minutes.

Serve on a well heated platter with steamed rice.

Szechuan 'Yu Hsiang' Pork Ribbons
Quick Fried with Shredded Vegetables

Steamed Pork with Ground Rice

Lion's Head

Steamed Pork with Ground Rice

1½ lbs pork tenderloin
1 tsp salt
2 tbsp soy sauce
2 tbsp Szechuan chilli bean paste
1 tsp sugar
3 slices ginger root, finely shredded
4 scallions, finely chopped
Freshly ground Szechuan pepper
1 tbsp oil
4 tbsp ground rice
1 lettuce of cabbage
sesame oil to garnish

Cut the pork into bite-sized slices. Marinate in salt, soy, chilli bean paste, sugar, ginger root, scallions, Szechuan pepper and oil, for 20 minutes. Coat each piece of pork with ground rice and arrange in neat layers on a bed of lettuce or cabbage in a steamer and steam vigorously for 25-30 minutes. Garnish with sesame oil, and more finely chopped scallions. Serve with chilli sauce as a dip if desired.

Lion's Head

2 lb ground pork butt
2 scallions, finely chopped
2 slices ginger root, finely chopped
2 tbsp pale dry sherry
2 tbsp cornstarch
1 tbsp lard
1 lb Chinese cabbage (bok choy), quartered length wise
1 cup chicken broth

Mix together the pork, scallions, ginger, sherry, cornstarch, and half the salt. Shape the mixture into six or eight meatballs. Melt the lard in a deep, flame proof pan. Add the cabbage and remaining salt, and fry for 30 seconds. Place the meatballs on the cabbage and pour the broth over the top. Bring to the boil, then cover tightly. Simmer gently for 30-40 minutes. Serve hot. (Alternatively the meatballs may be fried in a little lard with soy sauce and sugar, before placing them on top of the cabbage.)

Mongolian Lamb in Lettuce Puffs

1½ lb leg of lamb, boned
2 garlic cloves
2 slices ginger root
2 scallions
1 tbsp yellow bean paste
½ tsp 5 spice powder
2 tbsp pale dry sherry
1½ tbsp soy sauce

Cut the lamb into 2-3 large pieces. Mince the garlic, shred the ginger and scallion. Add them to the lamb with the yellow bean paste, 5 spice powder, sherry and soy sauce. Leave the lamb to marinate for 1 hour. Place the lamb in a heat proof basin. Insert into a steamer and steam for 1¼-1½ hours. Remove and drain. When ready to serve, heat 4 tbsp oil in a large frying pan or wok. Fry the lamb for 8-10 minutes until crispy. Cut the lamb across the grain into 2½" × 1" pieces. Serve wrapped in crispy lettuce leaves with 'Peking Duck' sauce.

Mongolian Lamb
Lettuce Puffs

Stir-fried Sliced Pork with Pig's Liver and Kidney

Crispy Noodles

Stir-fried Sliced Pork with Pig's Liver and Kidney

1 pig's kidney	1 tsp sugar
¼ lb lean pork loin	2) ½ tsp pepper
½ cup pig's liver	½ tsp vinegar
¼ cup snow peas	1 tsp cornstarch
6 water chestnuts	½ tsp salt
1) Marinade for pork, liver	½ tsp sugar
and kidney:	½ tsp sesame oil
1½ tbsp cooking wine	2 tbsp water
1½ tbsp soy sauce	1 tbsp shredded scallions
1½ tbsp cornstarch	

Soak the kidney overnight in cold water. Skin and core. Cut the pork, liver and kidney into thin slices. Divide marinade into 3 and marinate pork, liver and kidney separately for 30 minutes. Thinly shred the snow peas. Slice water-chestnuts. Mix 2) together. Set a 12″ wok over a high heat for 30 seconds. Pour in 4 tbsp oil. Heat until almost smoking, reduce heat slightly, stir in the pork, liver and kidney. Cook, stirring for 2-3 minutes. Remove with a slotted spoon. Add a further tbsp oil to the wok. Stir fry the snow peas and water-chestnuts for 1-2 minutes. Pour in 2). If the mixture becomes too thick add more water. Cook until it forms a thick, transparent paste then stir in the pork, liver and kidney. Add the scallions and transfer to a serving dish. Serve immediately.

Crispy Noodles: Serve with Stir-fry.

1 lb egg noodles	salt
oil for deep frying	sesame oil

Cook the noodles in 7 cups salted water for 12-1 minutes stirring occasionally. Drain well. Pat dr with absorbent paper.

Fry in hot oil for 2-3 minutes until very crisp Drain well. Sprinkle with salt and sesame oil.

Stir-fried Beef with Oyster Sauce

¾ lb lean beef	2 tsp cornstarch
Marinade:	2 tbsp oil
2 tsp white wine	1 cup broccoli
1 tbsp soy sauce	2 cups oil
½ tsp salt	2 tbsp oyster sauce
1 tsp sugar	½ tsp salt
¼ tsp baking powder	1 tsp sugar
¼ tsp pepper	2 tsp chopped scallions
1 tbsp water	

Cut the beef into thin 1″ squares. Marinate in all the marinade ingredients for several hours. Cook the broccoli in boiling salted water for 15-20 minutes. Drain Heat the 2 cups oil in a wok, stir-fry the marinated bee for 20 seconds. Remove beef with a slotted spoon Remove all but 4 tbsp oil from the wok. Stir fry the broccoli for 30 seconds. Add the beef, sprinkle with oyster sauce, salt, sugar, and chopped scallion. Stir fry for a further 30 seconds. Serve.

Stir-fried Beef
with Oyster Sauce

MEAT

Deep Fried Chicken with Lemon Slices

The Hainan 'Chicken Rice'

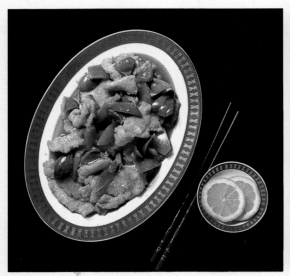

Deep Fried Chicken with Lemon Slices

3 lb chicken breast meat	6 tbsp light broth
1) ½ tsp salt	½ tsp salt
½ tbsp cooking wine	2 tbsp cornstarch
½ tbsp light soy sauce	1 tsp sesame oil
1 tbsp cornstarch	1 green capsicum, cored and
1 tbsp water	seeded.
1 egg yolk	1 red capsicum, cored and
black pepper	seeded.
2) 6 tbsp cornstarch	oil for deep frying
3 tbsp all-purpose flour	2 lemons thinly sliced
3) 3 tbsp sugar	chopped parsley
3 tbsp lemon juice	

Skin the chicken. Cut into bite-sized, thin slices. Marinate in 1) for 10 minutes. Mix 2) on a plate and coat each chicken piece with the flour mixture. Mix 3) in a small bowl. Cut capsicum into 1" pieces.

Place a 12" wok over a high heat. Heat the oil until almost smoking. Deep fry the chicken slices until golden brown. Remove with a slotted spoon to a heated plate. Pour off all but a tablespoon of oil. Stir fry the capsicum until it begins to brown. Pour in 3). Bring to the boil, stirring until thickened. Add the chicken pieces. Stir for a further few minutes. Transfer to a heated serving platter, and garnish with lemon slices and chopped parsley.

The Hainan 'Chicken Rice'

1 lb long-grain rice	3 slices ginger root
1 chicken, weighing 3 lb	3 tsp salt
¾ lb broccoli	¼ lb green peas
2 medium onions	

Cook the rice in boiling salted water until tender, drain. Bone the chicken and chop through the skin into 3 bite-sized pieces. Cut broccoli into same sized pieces. Thinly slice the onion.

Simmer the chicken in a large pan with 2½ pin water, the ginger, onion and salt, for about 50 minute or until the chicken is cooked. Remove the chicken skim away the excess fat from the broth. Add th broccoli and peas. Bring to the boil. Stir for a fe minutes. Finally add the rice, leave to cook gently for minutes or until the broth has been absorbed. Arrang the chicken pieces on top of the rice and vegetable Cover the pan to allow the chicken pieces to he through.

The chicken should be eaten dipped in soy sauce which has been added some garlic, scallion and sesam oil.

Szechuan Bang Bang Chicken

2 chicken breasts	½ tsp sugar
1 medium cucumber	¼ tsp salt
Sauce:	2 tsp broth
4 tbsp peanut butter	½ tsp chilli sauce
2 tsp sesame oil	

Simmer the chicken in a pan of water for 30 minutes. Remove the chicken breasts and cut them into ½" thick strips. Thinly slice the cucumber. Spread cucumber on large serving platter. Pile the shredded chicken on top Mix the peanut butter with the sesame oil, sugar, sa and broth. Pour the sauce evenly over the chicken Sprinkle the chilli sauce evenly over the top.

This is a good dish to serve as a starter. The diner should actually toss and mix the ingredients in the disl at the table themselves.

Szechuan Bang Bang
Chicken

POULTRY

Minced Squab with Oyster Sauce

Aromatic and Crispy Duck

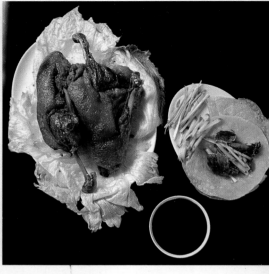

Minced Squab with Oyster Sauce

4 dried Chinese mushrooms	4 tbsp peanut oil
1 squab	1 tsp (shredded) ginger root
1 tbsp pale dry sherry	2 scallions
1 tbsp soy sauce	½ cup frozen peas
½ tsp sugar	½ cup chopped
½ tsp pepper	water-chestnuts
½ tsp salt	1 tsp cornstarch blended in
2 chicken livers	1tsp water
½ cup minced pork	2 tbsp oyster sauce
¼ cup rice noodles	1 large crisp lettuce

Soak the mushrooms in boiling water for 30 minutes. Finely shred the cap, discard the stem. Bone and skin the squab, shred the meat finely. Add sherry, soy sauce, sugar, pepper and salt to taste. Chop the chicken liver and mix with the minced pork. Stir into the squab. Deep fry the rice noodles until they turn white. Drain well on absorbent paper. Heat 3 tbsp oil in a large wok until it is almost smoking. Reduce heat to moderate, stir fry the ginger, scallion and peas for a few seconds. Add the pork, chicken liver and squab mixture. Stir over the heat for a few minutes. Remove to a bowl. Wipe the wok clean, heat the remaining oil, stir fry the chopped chestnuts and mushrooms with the salt for 1-2 minutes, return the squab mixture. Stir constantly for a further two minutes. Add the cornstarch mixture, stir well. Stir until lightly glazed, add oyster sauce, transfer to a heated serving platter. Arrange the crispy noodles around it with a few crisp lettuce leaves. It is customary to wrap the squab mixture in the lettuce leaves and roll up tightly to eat with the fingers.

Aromatic and Crispy Duck

1 duck, weighing 3½ lb.	½ tbsp 5 spice powder
2 tbsp black bean sauce	3 slices ginger root
2 tbsp dark soy sauce	

Rub the duck inside and out with the black bean sauce soy sauce, 5 spice powder and ginger. Leave in a coo place overnight. Insert the duck into a steamer, stear vigorously for 1½ hours. Drain and dry the duck. Dee fry the duck for 10-12 minutes until very crispy. Scrap the duck meat off the carcass. Roll up in pancakes wit shredded cucumber and scallions, and 'Duck Sauce The sauce is made with: 2 tbsp yellow bean sauce; 3 tbs, sugar; ½ pint water. Mix the three ingredients togethe bring to a boil, boil until the liquid is reduced by half. St in 3 tbsp sesame oil.

The Peking Duck

1 duck, weighing 4 lbs	Sauce:
½ medium cucumber	small can yellow bean sauce
4 scallions	3 tbsp sugar
	2 tbsp oil

Clean and dry the duck. Leave in a cool place overnigh Finely shred the cucumber and scallion. Preheat th oven to 400°F. Place the duck on a wire range set on to of a baking pan. Cook the duck for 1¼ hours. The duc should be very dark and crispy.

Sauce: Heat 2 tbsp oil in a small pan. Add the yello bean paste and sugar. Cook together for 1-2 minutes.

Serving and eating: Peel the skin off the duck. C into 2″ slices. Serve on a heated platter. Carve the me off the duck into 2″ slices, serve on a separate platte The duck skin and meat are eaten by wrapping them i pancakes which are first of all brushed with a tsp of 'duc sauce' and a layer of cucumber and scallion.

POULTRY

Stir Fried Chicken with Sliced Zuchini

Stir Fried Chicken with Sliced Zuchini

1½ lb chicken breast meat	pinch Vi-Chen
2 tsp cornstarch	¼ tsp pepper
1 egg white	½ lb zuchini
1 tbsp pale dry sherry	4 tbsp peanut oil
1 tsp salt	2 slices ginger root, shredded

Cut the chicken into thin slices. In a large bowl, mix the chicken with the cornstarch, egg white, sherry, salt, pepper and Vi-Chen. Drain. Cut the zuchini into thin slices.

Heat 3 tbsp oil in a wok with the ginger. Add the chicken, stir fry for 2 minutes until all the pieces have turned white. Transfer to a bowl. Wipe the wok clean, add another tbsp oil. Add the zuchini, stir fry for minutes, then transfer to a serving platter. Return the chicken to the wok, add the cornstarch mixture. Stir for a few seconds until a clear glaze is formed. Pour the contents of the wok into the middle of the zuchini. Serve at once.

Szechuan Chilli Chicken

POULTRY

Szechuan Chilli Chicken

¾ lb chicken breast meat	2 small dried chilli peppers
tsp salt	2 green/red capsicum
egg white	2 fresh chilli peppers
tbsp oil	2 tbsp soy sauce
½ tbsp cornstarch	2 tbsp wine vinegar
slices ginger root	

Cut the chicken into bite-sized pieces. Add the salt, egg white, 1 tbsp oil, and cornstarch. Mix and rub these evenly over the chicken pieces to form a thin coating.

Chop the ginger, and dried chilli. Cut the capsicum into bite-sized pieces. Heat the remaining oil in a wok. Add the ginger and chilli peppers stir fry for 1 minute. Add the chicken, separating them while stirring. Add the capsicum, soy sauce and vinegar, fry for a further 2 minutes. Serve immediately with steamed rice.

Quick Fried Chicken Cubes with Cashew Nuts

Deep Fried Boneless Duck

Quick Fried Chicken Cubes with Cashew Nuts

1 lb chicken breast meat	Sauce:
1 egg white	2 tbsp soy sauce
1 tbsp soy sauce	2 tsp vinegar
1 tbsp cornstarch	1 tbsp pale dry sherry
1 green capsicum	1 tsp cornstarch
1 red capsicum	½ tsp salt
3 scallions	2 tsp sugar
½ cup oil	
1 cup cashew nuts	
3 slices ginger root	

Cut chicken into bite-sized pieces. Add the egg white, soy sauce and cornstarch. Marinate for 30 minutes. Cut capsicums and scallions into 1″ pieces. Heat the oil in a wok. Add the cashew nuts. Fry over the heat for 1 minute. Remove and drain on absorbent paper. Remove all but 4 tbsp oil from the wok. Heat again, add chicken pieces. Stir fry for 1 minute. Remove and drain.

Add 2 tbsp oil to the wok. Over a high heat, add the ginger and scallion and capsicum. Fry quickly for 1 minute. Add all the ingredients for the sauce. Toss over the heat for 1 minute. Return the chicken, toss for 3-4 minutes, transfer to a heated serving platter. Return the wok to the heat, add the cashew nuts. Stir over a high heat. Remove and arrange them around the chicken mixture on the platter.

Deep Fried Boneless Duck

1 duck weighing 3½ lb	1½ cup beef broth
1 egg	4 cloves garlic
4 tbsp cornstarch	3 tsp 5-spice powder
2 tbsp all purpose flour	3-4 pieces anise oil for deep
½ cup soy sauce	frying

Simmer whole duck in a large pan of boiling water for 4-5 minutes. Drain. Mix egg, cornstarch and flour to a smooth batter.

Mix soy sauce, broth, garlic and 5-spice powder. Simmer with anise for 3-4 minutes in a large pan. Add duck. Coat well with sauce. Simmer for 40 minutes, turn bird over every 10 minutes. Remove duck, drain thoroughly. Remove the bones from the duck. Coat in batter mixture.

Deep fry the duck for 3-4 minutes, until very crispy. Cut into 2″ pieces. Arrange on a serving platter. Eat wrapped in crisp lettuce leaves with Peking Duck Sauce.

Stir Fried Minced Chicken on Crispy Noodles

½ lb chicken breast	2 tbsp soy sauce
2 slices cooked smoked ham	2 tbsp chicken broth
6 slices ginger root	1 tbsp vinegar
1 large onion	1 tbsp chilli oil
3 scallions	1 tsp sugar
3 tbsp oil	2 tsp cornstarch
½ tsp salt	

Mince chicken. Finely shred ham, ginger and onion. Slice scallions. Heat oil in a large frying pan. Add onion, ham and ginger. Stir-fry for 2 min. Add the minced chicken. Sprinkle with salt, soy sauce and broth. Stir-fry for a further 2 minutes. Add vinegar, sherry, chilli oil, sugar, scallions, and cornstarch blended with 2 tbsp water. Cook over high heat for 2 minutes.

Serve on a heated platter with crispy noodles, pancakes and a vegetable accompaniment.

Stir Fried Minced Chicken on Crispy Noodles

POULTRY

Peking Egg Battered Chicken with Beansprouts, in Onion and Garlic Sauce

Peking Egg Battered Chicken with Beansprouts, in Onion and Garlic Sauce.

3 breasts of chicken	2 scallions
salt and pepper	4 tbsp oil
2 eggs	4 tbsp broth
2 cloves garlic	vinegar to taste

Cut each chicken breast into 4″ slices. Rub with salt and pepper. Beat eggs lightly, and add the chicken slices to the eggs. Crush garlic and cut scallions into 1″ pieces. Heat the oil in the wok. Add the chicken pieces one by one, and reduce heat to low. Leave to sauté for 1-2 minutes. Once the eggs have set, sprinkle the chicken with garlic and scallion. Finally, add the broth and vinegar to taste. Simmer gently for 2 minutes.

Remove the chicken, cut each piece into small regular pieces, serve on a heated platter. Pour the remaining sauce from the pan over the chicken.

Boneless Duck with Eight Precious Stuffing

1 duck, weighing 5 lbs	2 scallions
1 duck gizzard	2 slices ginger root
1 tbsp chopped dried shrimps (soaked)	2 tbsp white wine
5 chinese mushrooms, (soaked)	2 tbsp soy sauce (light)
¼ lb cooked ham, diced	½ tsp salt
8 dried chestnuts (soaked)	pinch black pepper
20 lotus seeds, soaked and cleaned	3 cups cooked glutinous rice
2 tbsp oil	2 tbsp soy sauce (dark)
	1 tsp sugar

Clean the duck. Dice the duck gizzard, dried shrimps, mushrooms, and ham. Chop the chestnuts finely, peel off the lotus seed skins, remove the green central parts. Cook the lotus seeds and chestnuts in boiling water for 2-3 minutes until soft.

Heat 2 tbsp oil in a large pan, add the chopped scallion and ginger. Fry over a high heat for 1-2 minutes then add the mushrooms, lotus seeds, ham, shrimps and chestnuts. Stir in the wine, light soy sauce, salt and pepper. Off the heat, stir in the rice. Leave to cool. Pack the stuffing mixture into the cavity of the duck. Sew up securely. Brush the duck with the dark soy sauce and sugar. Place on a wire range set over a baking pan. Roast in a pre-heated over, 350°F for 1 hour. Slice the duck into large pieces to serve.

Boneless Duck with
Eight Precious Stuffing

POULTRY

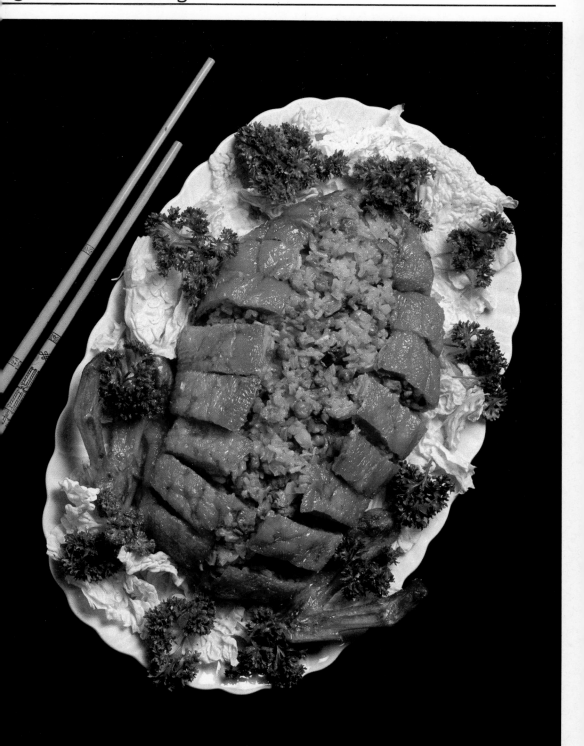

Quick Fry 'Crystal Prawns'

Baked Trout with Black Bean Sauce

Quick Fry 'Crystal Prawns'

1 lb fresh prawns	2 tsp chopped onion
1 egg white	½ tsp salt
1 tbsp cornstarch	1 tbsp pale dry sherry
6 tbsp oil	2 tbsp broth
1 tsp ginger root	½ tbsp vinegar

Clean, shell and de-vein the prawns. Mix together the egg white and cornstarch. Toss the prawns in this mixture to coat well. Heat the oil in a wok. Add the prawns. Stir fry over a low heat for 2-3 minutes until turning colour. Remove with a slotted spoon. Pour off any excess oil. Add the chopped ginger, onion, salt, sherry, and broth. Bring to the boil. Return the prawns. Stir over the heat for a few seconds. Sprinkle with vinegar. Serve.

Baked Trout with Black Bean Sauce

1½ lb trout (cleaned with head on)	½ tsp sugar
	1 tbsp light soy sauce
1) 1 tsp salt	1 tbsp pale dry sherry
½ tsp pepper	2 tbsp vegetable oil
½ tsp ground ginger	4) 1 tbsp shredded scallion
2) 2 tbsp shredded scallion	½ tbsp shredded ginger root
1 tbsp shredded ginger root	½ tbsp shredded red chilli
3) 1 tbsp black bean sauce	1 tbsp light soy sauce
1 tsp dried red chilli, chopped	1 tsp sesame oil

Lightly score the fish by making diagonal cuts at 1 intervals on both sides of the body. Rub it well with 1 inside and out. Lay the fish on a heatproof pan, arrang 2) on top. Heat the veg. oil in a small pan until almos smoking. Pour over the fish. Pour 3) slowly over the fish Cover tightly with foil. Cook at 400° for 15-20 minutes When cooked, pile 4) over the fish with the soy sauc and sesame oil.

Crouton Studded "pomegranate" crispy prawn balls

4 slices white bread	2 egg white
½ lb fillets white fish	2 slices ginger root
½ lb shrimp (fresh or frozen)	2 tbsp cornstarch
2 tsp salt	oil for deep frying
pepper to taste	

Remove crusts from the bread. Cut each slice into small crouton sized cubes. Dry in a hot oven until slightly browned. Spread out on a large tray. Chop the fish and shelled shrimps very finely. Mix together with the salt, pepper, egg white, finely chopped ginger, and cornstarch. Blend well. Shape the mixture into 2" balls Roll over the croutons to coat. Heat the oil in a deep fryer. Add the crouton studded prawn balls one by one Turn with a perforated spoon until evenly browned About 2 minutes. Remove and drain. Return to the oi for a further 1 minute frying. Drain well on kitchen paper. Serve with a good quality soy sauce, ketchup o chilli sauce as dips.

Crouton Studded "pomegranate"
crispy prawn balls

FISH

Deep Fried Sea Bass

Steamed Cabbage Rolls with Fish and Crab-Meat

Deep Fried Sea Bass

1½ lb sea bass	2 small chillis
3 tsp dark soy sauce	2 scallions
2 tbsp cornstarch	2 cups chicken broth
4 cups oil	2 tsp salt
¼ cup ground pork	¼ cup pickled cabbage,
1 slice ginger root	shredded
2 cloves garlic	2 tsp sesame oil

Clean the fish. Make diagonal cuts across the surface. Rub the soy sauce over the fish. Mix the cornstarch with 2 tbsp water to a smooth paste. Heat the oil in a wok, add the fish. When browned on both sides remove and drain. Remove all but 4 tbsp oil, reheat wok, add the pork, chopped garlic, chilli, scallion, ginger, broth, salt and pickled cabbage. Stir over the heat for 1-2 minutes. Return the fish, cook for a further 10 minutes. Remove fish to a heated platter. Stir the cornstarch mixture into the wok, add the sesame oil. Pour over the fish and serve.

Steamed Cabbage Rolls with Fish and Crab-Meat

8 large Chinese cabbage	1½ tsp salt
leaves	1 egg white
½ lb filleted white fish	1 tsp sesame oil
2 slices ginger root	½ lb crab meat

Pour boiling water over the cabbage to soften. Drain and dry well. Chop the fish coarsely. Finely chop the ginger. Place the fish and ginger in a bowl with the salt, egg white, sesame oil and crab meat. Mix well. Place 2 cabbage leaves on a flat surface. Put ⅛ fish mixture into the centre of each of the leaves. Roll the leaves up to form a tight roll. Place in a heatproof pan. Repeat until all the fish mixture has been used.

Insert the fish rolls into a steamer. Steam vigorously for 10-12 minutes. Place the cooked rolls on a heated platter and serve with soy sauce, and chilli sauce as dips.

Steamed Sea Bass

1 whole fish (about 1½ lb)	2 scallions
2 scallions	1½ tbsp soy sauce
1-2 slices bacon	1 tbsp pale dry sherry
Sauce and garnish:	3-4 slices ginger root
2 slices ginger root	1½ tbsp oil

Clean and gut the fish. Cut the scallions into 2″ pieces. Shred the bacon. For sauce and garnish; cut ginger and scallions into fine shreds. Mix soy sauce with sherry. Place fish on a heatproof dish. Spoon the scallion, ginger root and bacon shreds across the length of the fish. Insert the dish into a steamer and steam vigorously for 15-20 minutes. Remove the ginger, scallion and bacon from the fish.

Just before serving, pour the soy/sherry mixture over the fish. Garnish it with the shredded scallions and ginger. Heat the oil over a high heat until it is about to smoke. Pour the hot oil over the fish creating a loud sizzle. Serve at once.

Steamed
Sea Bass

FISH

Szechuan Fish Steak

Triple Fry of 'Three Sea Flavours'

Szechuan Fish Steak

1½ lb haddock	Oil for deep frying
2 tsp salt	½ cup chicken broth
2 tbsp cornstarch	3 tbsp soy sauce
1 egg	2 tbsp tomato paste
Sauce:	2 tbsp Hoisin sauce
1 large onion	1 tbsp sugar
2 cloves garlic	1 tbsp wine vinegar
3 slices ginger root	2 tbsp pale sherry
2 chilli peppers	
2 slices Szechuan Ja Chai	
pickle	
1 dried chilli	

Cut fish into 2″ × 1″ oblong pieces. Rub with salt. Blend the cornstarch with the egg. Dip the fish in the egg mixture to coat on both sides. Thinly slice the onion. Finely chop the garlic, ginger, chillis, pickle and dried chilli.

    Heat 4 tbsp oil in a large frying pan. Add the onion and other chopped vegetables, stir fry for 2 minutes. Add the broth, soy sauce, paste. Hoisin sauce, sugar, vinegar, and sherry. Stir them over a high heat until well reduced. Heat about 4 cups oil in a deep fryer. When hot, add the fish and fry for 2 minutes. Remove and drain. Place them in the pan of sauce. Simmer in the sauce for 5 minutes before serving.

Triple Fry of 'Three Sea Flavours'

¼ lb large prawns (shelled)	6 tbsp oil
4 scallops	1 tbsp soy sauce
¼ lb squid	3 tsp chilli sauce
4 tsp salted black beans	1 tbsp cornstarch blended
2 slices ginger root	with 3 tbsp water
2 scallions	1½ tsp sesame oil
2 cloves garlic	1 tbsp sherry
1 small red capsicum	salt and pepper

Chop the prawns, scallop and squid. Soak the black beans in warm water for 5 minutes. Drain, and finely chop. Shred the ginger root, cut the scallion into 1 pieces, chop the garlic. Cut the red capsicum into 1 pieces.

    Heat 4 tbsp oil in a large frying pan. Add the prawns scallop, and squid. Stir fry over a high heat for 1-? minutes. Remove with a slotted spoon. Pour remainin oil into the pan. Add the ginger, garlic and black beans Stir fry for 1 minute. Add the scallion and capsicum. Sti together over the heat. Add the broth. Cook for minute. Add the soy sauce and chilli sauce. Return th fish. Stir to blend with the sauce. Add the cornstarc mixture, sesame oil and sherry. Stir once more over high heat before serving.

Sesame Prawn Toasts

Crispy Seaweed

FISH

Sesame Prawn Toasts

cup pork fat	1 tbsp cornstarch
cup cooked shrimps	2 slices white bread
egg white	6 tbsp sesame seeds
alt and pepper to taste	oil for deep frying

inely chop pork fat and shrimps. Blend together well with egg white, salt, pepper and cornstarch. Spread the paste' thickly on the 2 slices of bread. Remove the rusts. Sprinkle the paste thickly with sesame seeds ressing them on well. Heat the oil. Lower one slice of read at a time into the hot oil, spread side down, for 2 inutes. Turn over and fry the other side for ½ minute. epeat for other slice of bread. Cut each 'Prawn Toast' in alf, then into finger sized strips. Serve hot.

Crispy Seaweed

2 lbs greens	½ tsp salt
4 tbsp split almonds	1½ tsp sugar
oil for deep frying	

With a very sharp knife, cut the greens into the finest shreds possible. Dry, by spreading them out on kitchen paper for ½ hour. Deep fry, or shallow fry the almonds until golden. Drain well. Heat the oil until it is about to smoke. Remove from the heat for ½ minute. Add all the shreds of greens. Stir and return pan to the heat and fry for 2-3 minutes. Remove and drain well. Serve on a well heated platter, sprinkled evenly with salt, sugar, and almonds.

Sweet and Sour Sliced Fish

Peking Sauté of Fish in Egg Batter with Garlic and Scallion

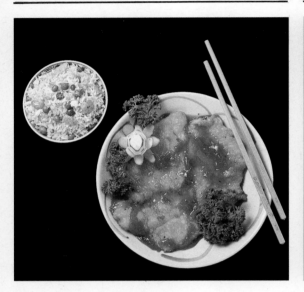

Sweet and Sour Sliced Fish

1 large plaice	sauce:
1 tsp salt	2 tbsp sugar
1 tbsp cornstarch	3 tbsp vinegar
2 eggs	2 tbsp broth
2 scallions	1 tbsp cornstarch
2 slices ginger root	(blended with 2 tbsp water)
2 cloves garlic, chopped	3 tbsp orange juice
6 tbsp oil	1 tbsp pale dry sherry
	1 tbsp soy sauce

Rub the fish with the salt and cornstarch. Beat eggs lightly, dip the fish to coat on both sides. Finely chop the scallion, ginger and garlic. Heat the oil in a large deep frying pan. Add the fish. Fry for 2 minutes on each side in the hot oil. Remove, drain well. Wipe the pan clean, add the sauce ingredients. Bring to the boil, simmer for 2 minutes. Return the fish to the sauce, simmer for a further 2 minutes. Serve immediately.

Peking Sauté of Fish in Egg Batter with Garlic and Scallion

1 large plaice, cleaned	2 cloves garlic
1 tsp salt	6 tbsp oil
1 tbsp cornstarch	½ tsp salt
2 eggs	5 tbsp chicken broth
2 scallions	1 tbsp pale dry sherry
2 slices ginger root	

Rub the fish with salt and cornstarch. Dip in the beaten eggs, to coat well on both sides. Finely chop the scallion, ginger and garlic.

Heat the oil in a large frying pan. Sauté the fish in the oil for 2 minutes on each side. Remove with a slotted spoon. Add the salt, scallion, ginger and garlic to the pan. Pour in the broth and sherry. Bring to a boil, return the fish. Simmer for 2-3 minutes. Transfer to a heated serving platter, and pour sauce over the fish. Serve immediately.

Cantonese Ginger and Onion Lobster

1½ lb Lobster (live)	½ tsp salt
4 slices ginger root	½ cup chicken stock
3 scallions	1½ tbsp soy sauce
oil for deep frying	2 tbsp pale dry sherry

Split the lobster in half through the head and tail along the centre line of the shell. Discard the grey sac in the head and the dark intestinal vein in the body. Chop into large, bite-sized pieces. Shred the ginger and chop the scallions.

Heat the oil in a deep fryer. When hot, add the lobster and cook, stirring for 3 minutes. Add ginger and scallions and salt. Cook for a further minute. Pour off the oil. Add the stock, soy sauce and sherry. Simmer for 3 minutes, stirring all the time. Transfer the lobster to a deep-sided serving dish. Pour the contents of the pan over the lobster and serve.

Cantonese Ginger and Onion Lobster

FISH

Stir Fried French Beans with Chilli

Braised Celery with Shrimps and Chinese Mushroom Sauce

Stir Fried French Beans with Chilli

1 lb French beans	1 tbsp light soy sauce
3 red chillis	½ tsp sugar
1½ tbsp oil	½ tsp sesame oil

Trim the beans. Wash, drain and halve. Cook in boiling, salted water for 2 minutes. Rinse in cold water, drain well. Shred chilli finely.

Heat the oil in a wok, add the beans, chilli, soy sauce and sugar. Stir fry for about 3 minutes. Add the sesame oil, remove from heat and serve immediately.

Braised Celery with Dried Shrimps and Chinese Mushroom Sauce.

10 medium sized Chinese mushrooms	2) 1 tbsp soy sauce
	½ tsp sugar
1½ lb Celery	1 tsp sesame oil
1) ½ cup chicken broth	½ tbsp soya oil
1 tsp salt	1 cup chicken broth
2 tbsp dried shrimps	3) 1½ tsp cornstarch
(presoaked)	1 tbsp water
	1 tbsp chopped scallions

Soak Chinese mushrooms in boiling water for at leas one hour. Cut off the hard stems before using. Wash an trim celery. Cut into 4″ long strips. Place in a ovenproof dish and pour in 1). Cover tightly. Cook a 375° for 30 minutes. While celery is cooking, pu mushrooms in a small saucepan with 2). Bring to a boi Simmer for 30 minutes. Pour in 3) and the liquid from the celery. Bring to the boil, stirring, to form a smoot sauce. Pour mushrooms over the celery. Sprinkl scallion over the top and serve.

Coral Cabbage

3 lbs Chinese cabbage	1½ tbsp dried shrimps
3 tbsp Red bean-curd cheese (and sauce)	(soaked and chopped)
	salt and pepper
2 tbsp tomato paste	2 tbsp butter
1 tbsp light soy sauce	1 cup chicken broth
4 tbsp oil	

Cut cabbage into 2″ pieces. Mix the cheese with th tomato paste, and soy sauce. Heat the oil in a large wol Add the shrimps and cabbage. Sprinkle with salt an pepper. Stir fry for 1-2 minutes. Add the cheese/so mixture. Stir the cabbage over the heat until well coate with sauce. Place in a deep baking pan. Add the butte Pour broth over the vegetables. Cook in a preheate oven 300°F for 45 minutes. Serve from the pan at th table.

Coral Cabbage

VEGETABLES

Spinach & Radish Salad

Spiced Bean Sprouts with Cucumber Shreds

Spinach & Radish Salad

1 bunch radishes
2 lbs spinach

Clean and trim the radish, flatten with the edge of a cleaver. Sprinkle with salt. Wash the spinach, remove stems. Place in a large pan. Pour over boiling water. Drain immediately and dry well. Sprinkle with 2 tsp light soy sauce, salt, pepper and pinch sugar. Toss the spinach with the radishes to serve.

Spiced Bean Sprouts with Cucumber Shreds

2 lb bean sprouts	1 tsp salt
½ cucumber	1 tbsp vinegar
½ cup dried shrimps	1½ tsp sesame oil
Sauce:	1 tsp sugar
1 tbsp soy sauce	

Wash bean sprouts. Thinly shred cucumber. Po▮ boiling water over beansprouts and drain well. Soa▮ dried shrimps in boiling water for half an hour. Dra▮ well. Mix together sauce ingredients. To serve, pla▮ cucumber on a serving dish with the beansprouts on to▮ then the dried shrimps. Pour the sauce over befo▮ serving.

The Buddhist's Delight

½ cup 'hair' seaweed
  (soaked)
3 tbsp pine nuts
8 Chinese mushrooms
  (soaked)

6 water-chestnuts
1½ cups Chinese cabbage
¼ cup bean curd skin, if
  available (soaked for 5
  minutes)

Place all the ingredients in a wok or deep pan. Add 1 cu▮ broth, 1 tsp salt, 1½ tbsp light soy sauce, 2 tbsp oil. Brin▮ to a boil. Simmer for 5 minutes. Add 1 tsp sesame o▮ and 1 tbsp cornstarch blended in 3 tbsp water. Bring to ▮ boil, simmer for 2 minutes. Serve in a bowl.

The Buddhist's Delight

VEGETABLES

Cold Tossed Bean Curd

Crispy Wontun with Sauce

Cold Tossed Bean Curd

3 cakes soy bean curd	1 tbsp sesame oil
1) 2 tbsp chopped Szechuan pickle	2 tbsp soy sauce
	salt
2 tbsp dried shrimps (soaked)	1 tbsp lemon juice
	1 tbsp chopped garlic
2 tbsp scallions, chopped	½ tbsp sugar
2) 3 tbsp oil	¼ tsp pepper

Dice the soy bean curd. Sprinkle 1) onto the curd. Pour in 2) mixed well. Leave to marinate for 1 hour. Chill to serve.

Crispy Wontun with Sauce

Crispy skins are readily available from most Chinese supermarkets. Wrap small amounts of stuffing in the skin and deep fry for 2-4 minutes until very crisp. To fill: place 1 tsp stuffing at the centre of the skin, fold corner to corner, press edges together well.

Stuffings: – may consist of ground pork with chopped shrimps added.

Sauce: – the sauce is usually a sweet & sour sauce which consists of mixing the following ingredients:

1 tbsp cornstarch	1 tbsp soy sauce
1 tbsp tomato paste	2 tbsp sugar
1 tbsp vinegar	1½ tbsp oil

Place all the sauce ingredients into a pan, stir together over medium heat for 4-5 minutes.

Egg Slices in Three Colours

3 eggs	½ tsp salt
3 preserved eggs	2 tbsp water
3 salted eggs	1 tbsp lard

Break the 3 eggs into a bowl. Mix with the salt, and water. Shell the preserved eggs, and salted eggs. Cut into ½" pieces. Mix with the beaten eggs. Coat the inside of a basin with the lard. Put the mixed eggs into it. Place in a steamer and steam for about 15 minutes.

Remove from steamer, leave to cool for 10-15 minutes. Cut into 1½" squares. Arrange on a flat serving platter.

Egg Slices in
Three Colours

FILLERS

Yangchow Special Fried Rice

Paotzu Steamed Buns with Pork, Cabbage and Mushrooms

Yangchow Special Fried Rice

Yangchow Special Fried Rice is one stage richer and more elaborate than ordinary fried rice. It is prepared simply by adding 3-4oz cooked pork and the same amount of shrimps to basic 'vegetable fried rice'. It should not only be abounding with natural flavour, it should also be richly savoury because of the added pork and shrimps.

Paotzu Steamed Buns with Pork, Cabbage and Mushrooms

3 cups self-raising flour	1 tbsp chopped ginger root
1 cup warm water	½ lb ground pork
1 tsp fresh yeast	1 tbsp salt
1 lb cabbage	1 tbsp soy sauce
6 black Chinese mushrooms, pre-soaked	1 tsp pepper
	1 tsp sesame oil

Place the flour in a large bowl. Sprinkle the yeast on the warm water, stir and leave for 10 minutes, until frothy. Add the liquid to the flour, stir well. Leave in a warm place for 2 hours or until doubled in size.

Chop the cabbage, mushrooms and ginger. Add the pork, soy sauce, pepper and sesame oil. Mix well.

Knead the dough for a few minutes. Cut into 1½" pieces. Press a little of the pork mixture into each piece of dough. Shape into small round buns. Leave for 15-20 minutes. Place in a steamer and steam vigorously for 10 minutes. Serve immediately.

South Sea Noodles

2 tbsp Chinese dried shrimps, soaked	garnish:
	½ lb shelled prawns
½ lb Chinese rice flour vermicelli	2 gloves garlic, chopped
	4 scallions, chopped
4 tbsp oil	1 tbsp soy sauce
2 medium onions, sliced	1 tbsp Hoisin sauce
4 bacon slices	1 tbsp pale dry sherry
2 tbsp curry powder	2 tbsp oil
salt	2 tbsp chopped parsley
½ cup chicken broth	

Drain the shrimps, chop. Cook the noodles in boiling water for 3 minutes, drain and rinse under cold water. Heat the oil in a wok, add the onion, chopped bacon and dried shrimp. Stir fry for 1 minute, add the curry powder and salt. Fry for a further 1 minute. Add the broth and noodles. Stir over the heat for 2-3 minutes. Transfer to a heated serving platter. For the garnish, heat the oil in a small pan, add garlic and prawns and stir fry over high heat for 1 minute. Add soy and Hoisin sauce, and sherry. Sprinkle with scallions and parsley. Pour on top of noodles to serve.

FILLERS

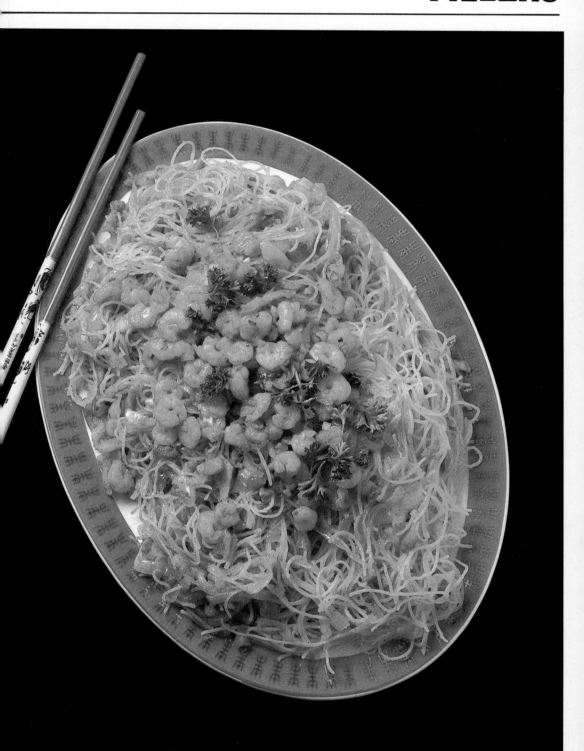

Mu Shu Rou

Mu Shu Rou

½ lb ground pork	3 scallions
3 tsp soy sauce	2 slices ginger root
2 tsp water	3 eggs
salt and pepper	1 tsp salt
2 tbsp 'wood ears'	5 tbsp oil
2 stalks 'golden needles'	1 tbsp pale dry sherry
4 dried Chinese mushrooms	

Mix pork with soy sauce, water, salt and pepper. Marinate for 10 minutes. Drain. Soak all the mushrooms in water for 15 minutes. Drain and shred. Shred the scallions, and ginger. Beat the eggs and the salt. Heat half the oil in a large frying pan. Add the mushrooms and ginger, stir over the heat for 1 minute. Add the pork, stir over the heat for 2 minutes. Add the scallion, stir and remove all the contents of the pan with a slotted spoon. Add the remaining oil to the pan. When hot pour in the beaten eggs. When the eggs have set return the removed contents. Stir to mix with egg. Sprinkle with sesame oil and sherry.

Serve wrapped in pancakes, or leaves of crisp lettuce.

Ma Po Tou FU

3 cakes bean curd	¼ lb ground beef
2 tbsp salted black beans	1 tsp salt
3 scallions	1 cup broth
3 cloves garlic	1 tbsp cornstarch
4 chilli peppers	1 tbsp soy sauce
3 tbsp oil	½ tsp pepper

Simmer the bean curd in water for 3 minutes. Drain and cut each cake into a dozen pieces. Soak the black bean in water for 20 minutes. Drain. Chop the scallions, garli and peppers.

Heat the oil in a large wok, add the beef, salt, and black beans. Stir over the heat for 3-4 minutes. Add the pepper, scallions and garlic. Fry for 2 minutes befor adding half the broth, and bean curd. Leave to simme for 4 minutes.

Mix the remaining broth with the cornstarch and so sauce. Pour into the wok. Bring to the boil, simmer fo 2-3 minutes. Sprinkle with pepper and serve with rice.

Ma Po Tou FU

FILLERS

Peking Onion Pancake

Cold Tossed Bean Curd with Cha Tsai Dried Shrimps

Peking Onion Pancake

3 cups all purpose flour	6 tbsp chopped onion
1 cup boiling water	3 tsp salt
1/3 cup cold water	5 tbsp oil

Place flour in a bowl. Gradually add boiling water, stirring all the time. Leave for 3 minutes. Stir in cold water. Knead well. Leave, covered, for 20 minutes. Divide into 6 pieces, roll into 6 large 10″ pancakes. Sprinkle each with chopped onion and salt. Tightly roll up each pancake. Twist into a coil. Press flat with palm of hand and roll to 1/4″ thick pancakes. Heat oil in a large frying pan. Fry the pancakes over a medium heat for 3 minutes on each side. Serve cut into wedges.

Cold Tossed Bean Curd with Cha Tsai Dried Shrimps

3 Tofu (soy bean curd)	2) 3 tbsp oil
1) 2 tbsp Szechuan pickle, chopped	2 tbsp light soy sauce
2 tbsp Cha Tsai dried shrimps	1 tbsp sesame oil
	1 tbsp lemon juice
2 tbsp chopped scallions	1 tbsp crushed garlic

Soak the shrimps in 2 tbsp white wine until softened. Chop finely. Dice the tofu. Place in a bowl. Sprinkle 1) on top of tofu. Leave for 5 minutes. Pour on 2). Mix well Serve chilled.

Quick Fried Snow Peas with Bean Sprouts

3/4 lb snow peas	1 lb beansprouts
1 large piece Tsa Chai Pickle (Szechuan)	2 tsp salt
4 tbsp oil	2 tsp sesame oil

Finely shred snow peas and Tsa Chai Pickle. Heat oil in a large wok. Add pickle and snow peas. Stir-fry for 2 minutes. Add beansprouts, salt and 3 tbsp water. Fry fo a further 2 minutes. Sprinkle with sesame oil and serve immediately.

Quick Fried Snow Peas with
Bean Sprouts

FILLERS

Eight Treasure Rice Pudding

Peking Toffee Apples

Eight Treasure Rice Pudding

1¼ cups glutinous or sweet pudding rice	1 × ½ lb can sweetened chestnut puree
3 tbsp lard	or 1 cup sweetened red bean paste
2 tbsp sugar	Syrup
15 dried red dates (jujubes), pitted	3 tbsp sugar
30 raisins	1¼ cups of cold water
10 walnut halves	1 tbsp cornstarch blended with 2 tbsp water
10 candied cherries	
10 pieces of candied angelica, chopped	

Place the rice in a saucepan, cover with water and bring to the boil. Reduce heat, cover tightly and cook for 15 minutes or until the water is absorbed. Add 2 tbsp of the lard and the sugar to the cooked rice. Mix well. Brush a 3¾ cup capacity steaming mould with the remaining lard. Cover the bottom and sides with a thin layer of the rice mixture. Gently press a layer of the fruit and nuts into the rice. Cover with another layer of rice, much thicker this time. Fill the centre with the chestnut puree or bean paste. Cover with remaining rice. Press gently to flatten the top. Cover with a pleated circle of waxed paper. Secure with string.

Steam the pudding for one hour. A few minutes before it is ready, make the syrup. dissolve the sugar in the water, bring to the boil. Stir in the cornstarch mixture and simmer gently until thickened. Invert the pudding onto a warmed serving platter, pour over the syrup and serve immediately.

Peking Toffee Apples

4 crisp apples	6 tbsp sugar
1 egg	3 tbsp oil
½ cup flour	3 tbsp syrup
oil for deep frying	

Peel, core and thickly slice the apples. Blend the egg flour and ½ cup water to make a smooth batter. Di each piece of apple in the batter. Deep fry the apple i the oil for 2-3 minutes. Drain. Heat the sugar, oil an 2 tbsp water in a pan over a low heat for 5 minutes. Ad the syrup, stir for a further 2 minutes. Add the appl pieces and stir slowly, covering each piece of apple wit syrup. Quickly spoon the hot, syrup-covered apple into a large bowl of iced water. Remove quickly an serve.

Steamed Pears in Honey

6 pears	3 tbsp honey
6 tbsp sugar	2 tbsp Creme de Menthe

Peel the pears leaving the stalks. Stand the pears in pan and cover with water. Simmer for 30 minute Sprinkle with sugar. Simmer for a further 5 minute Drain the pears reserving half the liquid. Chill th pears for 2 hours. Add the honey and the liquor of th reserved liquid stir until well blended. Serve the pea with the liquor sauce, and light cream.

Braised Aubergines

Hsing Jen Tou Fu (almond float)

Braised Aubergines

3 medium egg plants	2 tbsp pale dry sherry
½ cup broth	2 tbsp finely chopped
2 tbsp soy sauce	scallions
½ tsp sugar	

Cut egg plants in half, lengthwise. Lay cut side down in a large flat casserole. Pour over the broth, soy sauce, sugar and sherry. Cover tightly. Cook at 375°F for 1hr. Baste once during cooking time. Serve sprinkled with finely chopped scallions.

Hsing Jen Tou Fu (almond float)

2 tbsp gelatine	Syrup:
1¼ cups cold water	½ cup sugar
1½ cups milk	2 cups cold water
Almond extract	½ cup orange segments to
	garnish

In a large heatproof bowl, sprinkle the gelatine over ¼ cup cold water. Let it soften for 5 minutes. Bring the remaining water to the boil and stir into the gelatine. Stir until dissolved. Add the milk and almond extract. Pour the mixture into a flat 7½″ × 12″ dish. The custard should be about 1½″ thick. Chill for at least 3 hours, or until set.

Dissolve the sugar for the syrup in the water. Bring to the boil. Bubble until syrupy. Chill. With a sharp knife make diagonal cuts 1″ apart into the Almond Float. Repeat in the opposite direction to form diamond shaped pieces. Arrange with the orange segments in a serving bowl. Pour on the chilled syrup and serve.

Ice Mountain

1 large Honeydew melon	variety of fresh and canned fruit

This is simply serving a chilled fruit salad in a scooped out melon shell. Slice an inch off the top of a large melon and scoop out the inside of the fruit. Cut the scooped out pieces into regular shapes. Mix the pieces of melon with six or more types of canned and fresh fruit. Pack the melon with this mixture. Chill the melon for at least 2 hours. Serve with lots of crushed ice.

INDEX

The publishers would like to express their thanks to KEN LO'S KITCHEN at the CHINESE COOKERY SCHOOL for providing the facilities for photography, and to MRS. FEI, MRS. LIANG and DEH'TA HSIUNG who prepared the dishes. Photography by Ne? Sutherland.